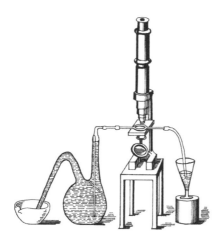

LIFE WITHOUT AIR

Daisy Lafarge

GRANTA

Granta Publications, 12 Addison Avenue, London W11 4QR

First published in Great Britain by Granta Books, 2020
Reprinted 2020

A CIP catalogue record for this book is available from
the British Library.

10 9 8 7 6 5 4 3 2

ISBN 978 1 78378 633 6
eISBN 978 1 78378 634 3

Typeset in Minion by Hamish Ironside

Printed and bound in Great Britain by T J Books Limited, Padstow

CONTENTS

∞

∞

You cannot solder an Abyss
With Air.

EMILY DICKINSON

Meridian
I dream in
I rid name
I mend air

Meridian
Marine id
Né midair
I drain me

Meridian
I'm in dear
Mired in a
Mined air

axiology

I woke up to the grating
        wrack of a mechanical sun,
it was ticking on its side
        just across the street, spun
off its great medieval wheels.
        There was weird light on our sheets
from the too-soon moon
        flung up in its place and held
there in cuckolded sky – I tried
        to wake you up but you only
curled in closer, murmured
        something about an animal
with heterochromic eyes.
        I went to make coffee and when
I came back you were stood
        at the window, staring at the sun,
naked as a plant, picking green
        from your nails like the verdigris
of God while the blind sky
        screeched on its broken axis
and the puce moon clotted
        with its carceral twin

The Daughter Channel

What's on the Daughter Channel
old bad goose? –
violet aggro, incarnadine sulk
a recitation from the Book of Lack

Half-baked breadcrumb
narratives
toed just-so
in the floorboard crack

So no one knows about prehistoric pain
or the Sapphic sky –

So what?

You'll just have to let the berries be berries
let them be eaten and shat

Stop moping by branches with glue sticks
        only fools try to put
                        old berries
back

Feed

Two men came by

possessed by opinions

a third performed

feats of avian

intervention

and cast the opinions

out of the men

and into the geese

that fed by the lake

and into the lake

that was an old idea

the demons sank

into and died in

the water

each opinion

a bubble

then a dark ring then

nothing

was left

of the men's ideas

what Genie got

She got it in the chest like the thump of Elijah,
awoke one morning to the trumpet
of her mother, its mouthpiece fused
to the notch above her sternum. All Genie knew
was that she woke up for school, and saw
the duvet rising sharply between her breasts,
its worn-out cotton an ascending minaret
that tugged itself back in reverence, declaring
the terrible instrument in matrilineal splendour.
Genie didn't touch or caress its tubulation,
but as she breathed out slowly the trumpet
started yelling so that cracks began to scale the walls,
each one spawning derivatives as she fought
with the trumpet for air. Genie held her breath
and the artex started raining.

The year processed in discord. Genie became adept
at the opposite of breathing and made very little sound
at all. But her mother's orchestra had other plans:
her gangs of woodwind would heckle from buildings
through menacing throats of gargoyles, while brassy-eyed
buttons of anonymous instruments winked like fish skins
from hedges. They always seemed to meet her
at the importunest of moments: on Saturdays spent working
at hotel wedding functions, when the sudden exhalation
of an untuned celesta might shatter her tray of champagne
flutes; or the time she tried to kiss Serina behind the privacy
of her locker, only to find it filled with cymbals,
stacked like dry stone making horizontal purdahs
of the sweetly staling air. It was only the one cymbal that slipped
out of line, but Serina backed away, unravelled

by its timbre. Genie was left in the reverberant air,
breathing in the lustful geometry
of lockers, the plasterboard walls of discoloured
posters and fading acne of blu tack, the fluids that flaked
off sticky-backed textbooks, particles from the prefabs
that rose in wet fields and found their way to her through commutes
of corridors, which offered themselves as half-bleached
sacraments, which Genie took in wholly.

> *And the ravens brought [her] bread and flesh in the morning, and*
> *bread and flesh in the evening, and [s]he drank of the brook.*

stag night in the embassy with Genie

& when the men woke up on the wrong
side of history, it was an unfamiliar feeling
they at first mistook for a hangover,
in the sick morning light of a breakfast bar
of a chain hotel, of average & ubiquitous luxury,
contemplating their actions of the night before,
nudging underbaked knobs of almond
croissants with incremental crumbs
of mirth. what none of them could recall
was how they'd ended the night in the embassy's
basement, inside a crate of flags, where they'd woken
whimpering, top and tail, that morning. the flags
had seemed plain enough the night before, but now each
of the men's cheeks were creased with the nondescript weft
of nylon, whose symbols of unknown nations showed no signs
of fading with time. the faces of the men bore puffy,
sheepish witness to a Commonwealth of Newfound Loyalties,
formed in the Overnight Scapes of Neutrality with slow & steady
Aqueous Agencies, by Genie who had lured them to the crate
which was also a front for the club she ran called Limbo

what we need is a story, they murmur, passing a small pot of jam between them. the men continue to murmur & pass the jam, the jar becoming thinner and thinner as their hands wear away the glass that turns back into sand (centuries!)

Which the men continue to pass as tight fistfuls of land
Which slip through their fingers & make filigree around their feet
That stacks into deposits
That grow into columns of increasing precarity & tower above the
     men
Who fail to look up as the towers collapse & brecciate their lungs
Which comes to be known as the Rapture of Alluvium

what Sister Weema avowed

Sister Weema sighs and takes off her glasses / the maze's edges blur into thickets. / *Rhododendrons*, she says, or something about capitalism; a hook / of stray ivy snags on her wimple. She sits / as composed as the air between bench slats, we lean back and listen / to the maze's shrieking. This maze is old, old as the wilderness / sifted for Pleasure: see the meritocratic fountains, the aspirational / hedges?

Lines of parents file into the maze. Before, they attest, down / payments on topiary were par for the course. But today they've brought children to learn / about concentrics: tulipomania cupping itself as fathers do time / in circles, pretending not to see as progeny dart through wattle, their flashes of analogue / skin that distend the winter-thin scrub. The blind man's bluff / has an adverse effect: the children go unseen for austerities of time.

Every so often Sister Weema burps. She says, / *If an eye is an organ that functions by light then what are leaves if not eyes? And think / how many are watching.* She breathes in deeply, her whole colony of skin. / Then, it seemed we were under surveillance: she jerks her cheekbone at the cypress in our periphery. *Shh!* / She says, *It's letting out gases to keep us sweet – we'd suffocate otherwise – / It's a total police state.*

The children meanwhile have outmanoeuvred / the maze. Crushing underfoot some other ways of seeing / that flake from their eyes like onion skins. The raw orbs guide them / to the outlying scrubs where they learn to gerrymander with tacit movements. The rhododendrons make / for shifty conurbations, you could hike the trail of sticky-fingered prospects where the children / meet, touch plastic, trade stocks in tchotchkes. They watch / them through the bracken, the parents roaming with armfuls of data. As the light / begins to fade, the children's names are called. They / trickle back into the maze – *There you are darling! You were hiding / so well!* By this time, the children have fought, become hedge-fund partners, fumbled at each other's bodies, named / all the animals.

Sister Weema's eyes roll back in her head and stick / there like two wet testaments.

Jennifer

Jennifer's not in
She's out looking for lichen
For the sliver with the best likeness
To her father's livered skin

mineral intimacy

unabashedly love
the minerals of you / I
always was a wind-fuckèd
gull for the White Cliffs pressd
hard & lithic between the lower elements
of yr lips / When u flay me w/ bracken its lust
is pre-floriferous / I used to sit awake in the beetling
dark to watch yr erosion 'til I stared so long tht fickle hair
fell deciduous 'round my shoulders & when I lookèd away my
lashes wer caught in yr layers & tore clean off like the stripping of bark /
Now prt of me's filed in yr endless strata & the wind combs hotly my nkd eyes

Dredging the Baotou Lake

Note: The Baotou Lake is a poisonous manmade lake outside Baotou, the largest industrial city in Inner Mongolia. It has been formed by the toxic by-products of rare-earth mineral mining, an industry that provides materials such as cerium and neodymium, which are needed for smartphones and flat-screen televisions, as well as green technologies such as wind turbines and solar panels.

1. The pipework of CERN

my love for you outstretches all the pipework of CERN
is a thing no one has ever said, most likely

but at least at CERN they understand that sometimes
you have to be your own knife

that the will to destruct, the unswervable
collision of self has its own imperative

no one accuses the atoms
of nihilism as they speed

through time and stale air
exploding the husks of each other

2. Matter

as with the moon, so with our mothers
it is what we make with the fallout that matters

3. Performing the border

we like to talk about our mothers
as we sip our fashionable drinks

and tease out the ecology
between emotions and handheld

devices; lest we forget
the screen of your phone

turned green from the night
you cried into its face, as though

the very pixels could impute
a body's affects, our to-and-fro

traipse from cyborg to goddess
and which were the hands of the woman

who built it? the ghost-handed
mother who says *there* and *there*

your hands come together to form their own peak
as the word *meniscus* arcs above the table

and crashes over the buzzing lunch-rush
room, the tiny bottles of cacao and ginseng washed

astray, counting for nothing. you are a single tear,
glued in the operating theatre. I am the serrated

dumb knife of *I know, I know.* the wave
breaks over its sutures. we look

elsewhere, at the backs
of our hands. our words step out raw

on the stage of ghost
fathers. we have both

been dreaming
of the toxic lake

4. Discharge

we would like to leave the city
but dread that first rip:
the needle pulled out of an arm too soon
the pale patient blinking in unmonitored sun

5. The ecology of beacons

on staggered green hills, the freakish spring
haar eats my steps with its breath
as if the sea's overhung
from the shit we have flung and then pant
to roll in like dogs

no light, no distance
the mist could hide anything
which is not the same
as forgiveness

only the scraggy corridors of gold
lead on like flight paths:
broom to the left, gorse to the right
when gorse goes out of season
love goes out of fashion
says your grandfather, a Fife man

half a thousand miles south
at my own end of this Lower Cretacean shtick
we call the gorse *firehills*
the fishermen more concerned
with warning than romance

6. Song of the ugly lake

have you ever festered
in your own quarantine, afraid
that your toxins would spread, only to find, when you finally
seep outside, that your sickness has turned benign,
as if the very air
could oxidise pain?

7. Terrestrial hazards

we have learned to distrust
both the shell
and its essence

this
is why we dredge
the Baotou Lake

sometimes
lightly drowning
sometimes

we surface, clutching
parts we hope
will prove uncuttable

8. Permaculture

my love for you will last until the sick lake
evaporates

is a thing there'll be no body
to speak to. else failing,

lay me down in a polytunnel
so the sky can make its own shallow sense.

let's set up camp around the lake
as we archive the whir of slowing organelles

watching the old-fashioned sun
as it sets on the field of our many tired eyes

afflection

if you find yourself canalling
in another's unconscious
or gondoliering back
through wild hoops of absence
rattling off some doggerel verse

swan if you must in a Venice
of the mind that wafts no
stench just the coolness
of words: impersonal,
lagoon, impersonal

The Salt and the Slug

Sunday, we sit in like weather
Wife says she didn't know about the salt
And the slug, she just knew about osmosis
That there are things it is vital to know
But moreso things to forget
That there are facts that go in
And those she pours out like so
Much salt on the slug

understudies for air

falsification air

what can I pass on, you ask,
about methods of detecting the air?
it has become so habitual
I am not sure where to begin.
each morning I walk into the world
looking for signs. early, before light
is normalised by the shadow of buildings
and the gentle fraying of traffic. it seems the signs
are most attracted to states of dereliction.
to receive them, it helps to be empty
but imbued with residual function
like a disused water tower
or any number of withering technologies.
lie back. let the world grow over you
like weeds. consider the sheets of air
gridlocked in double glazing. now
are you beginning to understand?

desecration air

the dunes migrate inwards, sag
like cellulite from the headland.
in birth, you grew maladaptive
breathing patterns to survive
the air, patterns in which you are now
architecturally invested;
your dealings with air are more frequent
than ever. brittle waves of grit
clump the wind-lashed marram
who only avoid the sand's smothering
by growing, syringe-like,
into the air, and in so doing suckle
and cleave the dunes around them.
such a boom and bust modality
raises the question of who
is mother to whom, if your method
of resisting an environment
becomes in turn the order
that generates its form

gaslit air

I was told to conduct
my body like an hourglass,
to stand on my head
and turn the blood cells
regularly. the sky throbbed
sideways like a haemorrhage.
soon I became one
with my public face, hid
fragments in the small print
of undergrowth, chastised
them for not being whole

attempted diagnosis air

your designs to fabricate an alarm
to apprehend the air
went through several prototypes, one of which
comprised an attempt to monitor tone
of voice: it was not *what* people said but the *way*
they said it, you tried to explain. it was both easier
and harder to test this approach with relatives
as they all tended to speak at once, even
when none of them were present.
there was, however, the thorny matter
of consent and feedback forms, by which the majority
of relatives were perplexed. in the end,
you left the forms in the airing cupboard
to let the air fill out itself; it acquiesced
in many hands of mould, dust and heat,
none of which you could hope to translate

asbestos air

lichen and moss
grooming your body;
it is a relief to watch
things grow without
difficulty

infrastructure air

the twin lines of naming and being
run parallel but never touch, true;
though no fresh reckoning for what grows
between the tracks and pleat the drowsing
slipstream: aramid heartsease, bitumen wrack;
seed heads bejewel the municipal
depots. what creed or council
could find it in themselves
to admit the air as parasite?
and if the ground falls away, it is still always air
pent between the lines, a chain-throat
contaminant of life. its fingers pollinate,
cleave down the gullet and throng
the dark thickets of lung. you wake with a breath,
already hooked, the trees haul you on as passive enablers

aggregate air

what immunity for
buildings against their
uprooting; city skins
grown thick with corporate
heraldry, scabbing the air
tight to wound. on every corner a tree
articulates its script, whole flyovers
cracked with growing pains.
for a short while we considered
talking cures: a vernacular for pipelines,
circuitry, the fetid grids and systems.
we soiled our mouths to mimic
the good fettle of root and seed.
waited quietly for the rains

eclosion air

the husks were everywhere, but still no one knew
what they were supposed to have emerged
from. the world had fallen from its pedestal,
and in its place left a globular question
around what had always been. the question
shimmered, gave off a scent of sulphur, and
could only be approached at ecliptic conjunctions
of two or more bright objects. some things
stayed the same: the smell of cordite, shadows
of hands dancing over coffee tables, the walk-of-shame
lino in staff kitchens, the smutting of dun-colour set
into pavements, as if the asphalt were filled with seeds.
you could even look someone in the eyes
and tell them, as before, 'I love you', but the words
would breach in the air between, haplessly
smearing the root

billabong air

how many labours exhumed from mud
to clarify the curve of the argument?
avoiding my lyric profligacy, I
won't go into which one, save to say
that it's what you remember, with a terrestrial
thump back to your body, when woken
halfway through a dream. the shock
of that bone and hair centrifuge. we all
knew what the rotation would take:
where one side began and the other
ended, where it went in between. some
stalled in havens where the argument oxbowed;
they knew it wasn't safe, but lay
down to rest in the wetland. we had
no choice but to sail on downriver.
I still think of them, their clod eyes
roiled with fever, churning the peat
of a stagnant loop

false alarm air

I once passed a high-rise
as an alarm began to sound. for a while,
there was no movement, and then an elderly lady
emerged from the front door, flapping across the lawn
in a single white towel. she was naked otherwise, still
dripping from her shower, a sea-green bottle of detergent
in hand. each of her limbs a sprig of pale lavender, protruding
in a gesture of genteel and outmoded frailty. we stared at
the building, its indifferent gaze, as the siren cut out quick.
the towel billowed round her body, a flag
to safer days. I glimpsed the podzol
belly, the mildew thighs. I was about to walk on
when she held out her hand, turned two eyes of cracked
china, and said: one day I will know how it feels
to haul around a body of rotting flowers, to let memory
chew holes in my mind like maggots. then she laughed, and started
to sing a song whose words were lost to the wail
of a younger alarm, just beginning to teethe

parasite climax

the clouds are polyamorous
wanting one and both

an earworm's auto-eroticism
rubs a brain against itself

a woman self-seeds
her elements through the city

wondering if the species
that didn't emerge

live on as contrails
of alignment

currents of the possible
and possible not;

gutless borers of the world
dig on

nothingness is the scene of wild activity

i

the electron
touch not yrself!
lest you reabsorb the energy of yr own photon, with silky caress
'o that is immoral!' says the male physicist, 'and yet the electron does it'
eyeing a particular pleasure w/ globular disdain
there *is* no void, unless the gesture towards the self is empty
a vacuum sac of touch & go   *cul!*
'the electron touches itself, ∴ touches everyone' says the physicienne
'batshit!' says the audience member
who does not like to be touched
by so fertile a substance

ii

as we have seen
repulsion is the core of attraction
the thing 'touched' is the thing
closest, pushed away;
noli me –
kin and bedmates
polarised

iii

on a yellow car called Sheila
rusting, it is easy to mistake the phallus
for horizontal lightning over Sussex
we called it 'dragon'
(what a flunk)
all I didn't know
was the sky thrashed like a drown fish
was not passive ground
but charged earth planing up
avenue desire

iv

the step leader pedals
her embryonic lathe
a face flares out
on the surface of an egg;
idle impasto lack

ghosted

Like everyone else, ghosts just want to be listened to. When I point out my ghosts someone says, oh, so-and-so flesh-and-blood? And I say no, no. What appears ghostly to you may keep up appearances with others. The ghosts' main problems are being so equivocal, and blowsy.

∞

My love is too full of good bacteria; good in abundance is bad. Bacteria are known to target already-compromised organisms and my love is always-already compromised, so it is always under attack. Lions rejected and cast out by their pride are the first to fall victim to disease and infection – of the eye, of the paw, of the so-called lion's pride.

∞

Ghosting is not an action performed by ghosts, it breeds them. Colonies of after-affects clump and overburden the ghosted's resources. In ghosting, the ghost removes itself from recuperable discourse; the ghosted's ear is deafened by the ghost's reverberating absence. The ghost's 'absence' is only a quotation of absence; ghosting is better understood as negative presence, the sticky residue of intimacy redacted. What results from this lack of closure between presence and absence, life and death, is emotional ectoplasm.

∞

Symptoms of emotional ectoplasm include: intermittent slime-states and chronic abjection. If you have been living with ectoplasm and believed it was yours, reconsider; ectoplasm forms solely in relation. If you experience ectoplasm while living alone, it is likely you are clogged with historic deposits.

∞

To accept memory as normalised haunting is to throw yourself to the ghosts. Haunting is the word you give when you cannot accommodate a tragic paradox. That it happened, that it is not happening any more but it happens *in* you in psychic real time, and you go under again and again. I must speak of it as substance to make you see; only in the realm of tragic paradox can all these arrows fly simultaneously true.

∞

Ghosting is presence-in-denial cashing in on absence. So-called trace-lessness is an acutely agonising, inarticulate presence. The production of ectoplasm is governed by an active-passive dynamic; the ghost is active and the ghosted passive; the ectoplasmic deposit accrues more generally in the passive. Ghosting is the faux-edit that leaves you imploring *stet* to an empty room.

∞

You have ingested a siege modality; you perceive your pain as a castle assailed by ghosts, a movement from outside to in. 'They' are not 'you'. But the castle is a ghost castle built by ghosts, with ghost mortar and ghost stone. The metaphors mix until I can no longer tell what's vapour, what's body. The ghosts leave traces, intestinal architectures. We touch, commune, absent each other. The ghosted just want to be listened to, too.

wifedom as triage of pleats & timeliness

she's down on the floor by way of a pretty phrase.
it is not the day to think of how buildings get built.
she can no longer be considered detached as a gable end.

like a shared roof, she has implications
and is implicated

Fossil Dinner

Enter my husband, most lauded cartographer of our day.

Who truly loves nothing more than hosting his colleagues for dinner, where they can relax and talk department and eat the flesh of animals.

Or perhaps loves nothing more than the exhibition of our tablecloth, which I spend my time mending and amending: a thick map of his design woven with silk and sendaline, landforms of millefleurs stuccoed green and gold, seaforms pricked with taffeta asters. The borders drawn blackly in thread.

My role at the dinners is to mind the cloth and not to speak. To be present, so to speak.

This evening all is de rigueur. There is food on the landmasses and wine on the estuaries. My husband and his colleagues talk of sprezzatura and deep time, of a man called Marianus.

As usual, Erik the palaeontologist takes advantage of the table's subterranea and puts his hand on my knee, talking loudly of his proclivity for layers while I sit still as a fossil, i.e. vibrating furiously.

Fürchtegott the theologian is more composed; he holds forth about ecclesia and the hot bun of Christ. Tonight there's a papery crust around his mouth like yeast.

My husband contends. He passes his hand over a nearby tundra and asks, is creation not a vesture; does the world not accentuate God the way a dress hints at a woman's divine curvature?

The moment is punctured by the arrival of the langoustine.

I raise my eyes from the tablecloth and drop my mouth:

The poor dish looks just like me.

I become aware of breathing heavily; my breath comes out in clouds over the territory and each one leaves a contrail, stinking softly of feathers.

The clouds segue on the far side of the table and begin to rain formic acid over the crudités.

No one speaks as an atmosphere pulls itself together.

My husband the cartographer becomes annoyed; he is disinclined to weather. The excess moisture begins to crease the cloth and his attempts to smooth it down simply make the folds migrate and reassemble elsewhere.

I gulp down the clouds and try to smile in a way that conveys *don't worry darling, it's simply the appearance and reappearance of form* –

. . . his left hand turns white from its grip on the fish knife . . .

At a loss I open my mouth and point at it, meaning, *the natural world is in here* –

But it's too late. Erik comes for my left arm and Fürchtegott for my right; they push my head down and my husband the cartographer lifts the tablecloth up over me, forcing me under on all fours as the dishes and aperitifs clatter away from my terrible orogeny –

Soon my eyes adjust to the underseas and counter-earths and the reverse stitching of territories.

From somewhere above comes the muffled voice of my husband, apologising . . . *you see, she is vulnerable and subject to historical flux* . . .

Erik replies that the discourse is the backdrop.

Fürchtegott says the meaning won't stand for itself.

Life Without Air

Empedocles was a woman
in a sex of natural disasters

Marmoreal she-throat, her of the little animals
who gathered in her side-vents before she burned

At fourteen she stood on the rim of the crater
but could only remember the railings

And when she inhaled clouds of perlite
felt them curdle her blood, becoming thought:

Floor is lava; eyes are algae;
ash is rock trying to become air

This is how she came to believe
in the oracle of necessity

She wrote of nature and purification in verse
of Attic nights and table talk

She wrote that trees are the favouritism of air
and that tall ones lay eggs: the olive and the medlar

She examined her embryos
and called the soft parts *lambkins*

She told everyone her name meant 'belly'
swore she saw best with smoke in her eyes

In the blood are the thoughts
and in the thoughts blended breath

Thus, when Empedocles saw rhodophyta streaming between her legs
    in the bath
it was blood-on-the-tongue doxology

Her students had other ideas, handing in essays
with *OED* definitions of 'soul'

And discourses on the blackness of water
without having once gotten wet

In the feedback sessions
Empedocles endeavoured to be patient:

† Whenever † the valves of the sea peach
are plucked by the current

Which is the earth sweating
its flammable raiment

Remember that air
is just fire waiting to happen

But her students were tidally fickle
rolling their eyes like any old element

She had wanted to tell them
of spume and anoxic waters

Of congeries of burnt women
waxing bacterial

That for a woman to survive
and keep surviving

Is extremophilia: waiting for language
to culture her like agar

When they came for the heretic Empedocles
she was already in her element:

Discoursing from ash on blood and air
and the reciprocity of the nipple

Exhaling with fumarolic dissent
that to be in your element is to die in it

p value

We'd been emailing about insects. It had begun with the inhabitants of our houseplants – aphids, fungus gnats. On the surface our concerns were purely domestic. But when asked *where do they come from?* it was obvious that neither of us cared about pest control. Instead we were unhealthily curious about the insect–plant relationship. *Was it destructive?* we wondered, *or co-dependent?* Our stewardship of the plants made us spectators of their demise. There had to be gainers and losers; we craved the details shamelessly.

I'd been writing about parasites. In the section of my ecology textbook titled SYMBIOTIC RELATIONSHIPS there were demarcated subheadings: mutualism, commensalism, parasitism. I had to keep reminding myself that parasitism was a type of symbiotic relationship, not its opposite. That 'symbiosis' wasn't a synonym for ecological harmony. I wondered if the people who kept using the s-word in exhibition blurbs and event descriptions knew what kinds of relationships they were endorsing.

You'd been thinking about angler fish. For years the male of the species was believed to be a parasite, who, born with the bare minimum of sensory organs, can only mature sexually once attached to a female. The unformed male clings to the underside of his mate and injects an enzyme into her that enables procreation. This same enzyme then dissolves the male down to his sex organ. Fertilised, the female carries around the shelled husk of the male on her body. I wondered if the female is conscious of the male's role in her conception, or does she experience herself as parthenogenic? It seemed to me that the parable of the angler fish was concerned with resplendent hybridity.

She'd been looking about for an explanation. A phylogenetic tree that could neatly classify her feelings and thoughts, fears and desires. It would be a system with an index and a glossary, a list of illustrations. That way she could easily verify what kind of relationship she was in, rather than this aimless swimming through textbooks, failing to locate a phylum to anchor to her mood. Someone had suggested to her that lack was an edgeless edge, constantly remade by motive forces of desire. She thought about the incompatibility of two sponges, each one trying to soak the other up. Then she tried to think of the word for a relationship where neither organism benefits. Perhaps this was so ubiquitous that it didn't need a term? She thought about the white space between the lines in her textbook, how much still lurked there, waiting to be boxed into terminology.

They'd been dreaming about pepper maggots and overripe fruit. It had come up because of the zombie worms. They'd been reading about *whale fall*, the resting place of a whale who dies at sea, the slow decomposition of its body on the ocean floor. The zombie worms mate inside the whale bones, then eat them. *Does a whale drop dead mid-swim?* they wondered. They'd read that the alternative to whale fall was washing up on a beach. Out of water, the whale's heat-conserving blubber becomes a furnace. They didn't know which was worse – zombie worms, or boiling alive inside your own heat reserves.

A few evenings earlier she'd been out walking on the hill and found a dead bee in the middle of the path. She knelt down and picked it up by the papery wings, gently prodded a finger over its body. Soft, surprisingly sturdy. *Did the bee drop dead in the middle of its flight?* The idea of a sting drifted across her mind, which she dismissed, because the act of stinging was surely what had caused the bee to die. She had believed unquestioningly since childhood that a bee's sting was its Achilles heel, and conferred on the species a benignity that set them apart from wasps, who stung with pagan abandon. But things didn't seem so simple any more. Doubt ebbed through her fingers and her interaction with the bee, a tentative holding which was over and underwritten by her thoughts, which – like wasps – weren't to be trusted.

At home she wrote in the back of her textbook:

the mind is the body's parasite

And she
resolved
to dispose
responsibl
y of her
pesticides.

throttle song

'she wants' to be more like moonlight
or a sky filled with porcelain
as it cracks under skittish weight
and bleeds the rosy milk of planets

'she wants' the old song with dirty words
and dirty, old-sung hands
that orbit her throat
as she barks red and white
at the sky, 'does she?'

How to leave a marriage

To begin with I watched the dentist's
receptionist select a four-hour video
of sea turtles on YouTube. It was a minor
lesson in vapid pacifism for the waiting room,
while lesser pain waited calmly in machines
of the neighbouring rooms. I composed
many emails, and emails arrived from friends
like soft rain. From the city I contemplated
the tenacity of peatland, and marvelled at plants
endemic to bogs. Meantime the fuchsias grew
fatter, the innards of eclairs sopping over, summer
abundance of lipids. I couldn't go near them
and crossed the road with my nostrils
aborted; I was done dying under banners
for sensations that weren't mine. I was trying
to remember the stages of putrefaction. Once
an ex-friend criticised another for always writing
the same poem, which wasn't meant kindly
but became a kind of anointing. All this
and more was coming up with the fuchsias
like sweet bile. I was at the mercy of merycism
and momentarily happy, walking the hills three
hours a day, just to ruminate. Consciously or not
asking the leaves how to undo a life, but
the moral thus far is that the colour green
can't devolve an ego back to its bare cells, no
matter how viscid you feel. It's more parasitic,
as Weil said of divine love, another mother's
eggs laid in you so you have to keep coming back
to feed them, and that's how we all get vicariously
fed. Colour is what we are visited by. Ovipositing,

I waggled my doubt beneath a family of magpies.
Didn't count them because I feared nuclearity and
moreso the gauzy bloom of consciousness, mine
or anyone's. Don't you ever feel like evolution over-
cooked. On the 12th day I reached the labyrinth
on the side of the hill, long grassed over, so you can't
see your options, let alone the way. The sun was stamping
symbols of bygone industry behind my eyelids,
solar hammer and anvil, solar shovel and smog.
The insects were all flying west, away from the sputum
they flung from. I took notes, which the insects duly
amended. I had stopped worrying about analogy
because when he said we are flies sprung from the carcass
of the universe, I knew he meant it. He'd found a way to listen
to the grasses self-seeded in the crown of his head,
no shitting. I thought if I talked to him long enough
maybe I would too, though I was wary of men and hoped
I would be forever, however grassy. It's not figurative
to believe that the seasons drip-feed us teleology.
Romance is the hole we're tripped into filling.
Love is the name we gave it.

I pulled many plants up by their roots, and the sap from the roots was
     sour.
I staked my alignment with the organically bitter.
I walked past the bushes panting, I mean, the bushes were panting,
and the clouds went crimeless with acrimony.

corymb & panicle

Buddleia didn't like her name
so I tore her a new one

everywhere the smell of opulent
summer and ring-doves moaning

plants that flower straight
from their stems so stubborn

even botany has a name
for the plural of incest

dog rose duende

like all asymmetrical creatures
we love from a lack of alternatives
and since a home can be made of any old where
I might have lived forever in your bottom drawer
becoming obedient as you were
to the god of dirigible wounds and ink pots
ecstatic with thumbs stuck in yellow and blue
disbelieving in colour while recipes
got rained down for dinner I mean
really, we had to eat the lists
and after the rain, whole heads of eglantine
who peered out from hedges with faces of bread

you can ingest a word to check on its edges
but might not be able to stop
to see if an organ's metabolic harmony
is just the deal it has struck
between the viscera's sibling rivalries

and so we learn to laugh at appalling
separation, because it isn't true
because deadheads grow back
after a season of salt grit
and an excision or two

                              this was the dance in your mouth and mine
                                a house cleaved in two at the end of a love
                           when neither could bear to look at the other
                               and so turned to stitch up the membrane
                                 between, diaphanous castle that love
                                   laid to siege, laid then a new wall
                                            and doppelganger stairs
                                              which already narrow
                                             they could only descend
                                            twinned in the updraft
                                             of rootless impressions
                                                   or listening ears
                                             turned to the wind

A Question for Zeno

    Dear Zeno
a paradox has been bothering me
concerning my rent and the love I rented out
to a miscreant landlord of the heart
Zeno say if I recently left a coercive relationship
and now spend two thirds of what I earn a month on rent
which admittedly is more than I can afford
but I like the feel of where I live
in the old ballroom of a whisky merchant
no doubt haunted by thwarted debutantes
treading the floorboards doused in morally
dubious nineteenth-century light
with its condensation (sensational!) mould
which gives me the perpetual notion of bliss
of living inside a chess piece
    Dear Zeno
I haven't got to the paradox yet
the paradox is that I would maybe have been able to afford this
on the monthly stipend so generously mine for a finite amount of time
for a thoroughly Enlightenment studentship
paid for by the estates of Lord Kelvin and Adam Smith
the benefactors of which believe I will do something interdisciplinary
with the time but little do said benefactors know
I don't have one discipline to rub against another
and were I to meet Lord Kelvin or Adam Smith
I doubt very much that I could be duly dutiful
but I would put it to you (and them)
that you can't be ungrateful if you've never been a daughter
and I have to admit that I have this whole time
frittered away my funded interdisciplinarity
on supporting a man, ████████████████

my X, who just redirected a letter from his mortgage company
to me, requiring me to pay for a flat I have not lived in for four months
and which he expects me to pay for indefinitely
and the paradox, Zeno
is that when I add this additional four hundred and twelve pounds
    a month
to my rent it exceeds my stipend, Zeno
beyond which I have no savings because my savings were all given
to the X of my X
(to pay his debt) two years ago
and yes people expressed dismay and concern
when I did this but it was because I loved and I trusted, Zeno
I was in love and I was in trust
and I believed in those things as a metaphysical force
    Zeno, I believe you know where I'm coming from
don't we both believe in the balance of Love and Strife
I speak from inside the mouth of Strife
because I so fully and foolishly licked the lips of Love
or what I thought was Love, which was the fulmination of my trust,
    Dear Zeno
I am walking to buy some vegetables.
Which seems an absurdity knowing that
unless this man who claimed to love me
(and yet has never had a job) sees some sense –
I won't make the next month's rent.
    Dear Zeno, I don't mean to be melodramatic
I know my problems are relative and minor
but I am consulting you as opposed to the good god
of my evangelical girlhood
or the bad god of my post-evangelical dispersals

who yesterday I almost called on because on examining
the exit wounds of my X's demands of me
I found at their edges some misplaced belief
in a sense of divine justice and providence –
who will hold him to account
if not the law or me?

Zeno, I know you are pre-salvational
but I believe you believe in a kind of balance
and, if I have understood correctly, in the virtue of paradox
and it is in this state of almost euphoric dissolution
that I crawl through November's mulch and ask you, Zeno
to cure me of this will to solve

Dear Zeno
In the vegetable aisle just now I saw the wife of a man I know
who is friends with my X, at least in the online sense,
her baby just a month or so old was strapped to her chest
and I walked towards her saying 'hello!'
having bumped into her just before the baby was born
and I had just moved back to this city, and we were polite and
    friendly then
when it was warm enough to stand and talk on the street
but just now she didn't say hello back and quickly walked past me
glancing with such total fear in her eyes or maybe just misrecognition
but I have to admit I worried, after these last weeks' cascade of lawyers'
emails and scatological talismans, whether I had been judged by the
    world
and been found lacking
    Dear Zeno, in lieu of children
it seems we have been fighting over the custody of emotions

    Dear Zeno

it should also be said that I don't wish to obfuscate

when I say the X of my X

I don't mean the X of a formula

(would that this were a simple equation)

    Dear Zeno, there must be some god or algebra somewhere I can
        propitiate

    Dear Zeno, yes, I admit I have benefitted

from the competitive economy of poetry and prizes

and I wonder in the Pre-Socratic logic that must for sure

be governing this prosopopoeial fiscal ecology

whether this is the nadir of the arc from which I benefitted

and for which I now duly atone:

please accept these karmic feet

forgive me for my love to eat

and live inside a chess piece

and love the dog

who bites the hand

who is the hand that bites

the poem I tried to write

that whole time but

couldn't because I thought

the feet had left me but really

living with him meant they were pushed

so far down inside they became

a kind of teeth that ate

me from the inside

    Zeno –

I can't help but tell you this in cadence

it is the only way I know

now the teeth are falling

out like toothwort I am all
fruiting body bleeding ears it is
not a good idea to touch me
during this season it is
I realise
vulnerability Friday
and I am ill-equipped
and in keeping with my will not to obfuscate
which I imagine will only heed
the presencing of this paradox
I have spent these past weeks trying
to convince my students of the distance
between the poet and the speaker

. . .

so if they bury me under this
complicit ellipsis
know that I deserve it

. . .

this is why I call on you to cap me
within the paradox's phraseology
I need a structural framework
to be corseted into strophe
and anti-strophe
pin me into
some kind of prosody
I have been marking essays with burst vessels
from the stress of this man in my body
who abused me with a metabolism I fed
with the 'profit' of my poetry
I can't stand to think of my poetry
running through the veins of a man whose depravity

I can't bring myself to understand
in which poetry is both the sieve
and the hand that slaps me free
to drain the blood back into sensibility –
maybe there is no bloodless poetry

        Dear Zeno
I am speaking this all into my broken phone's voice recorder
because I am beginning to think that the voice
is the last thing he can't take from me
        Dear Zeno
if he makes me sign away my right to write
about it (perhaps he will)
even though that constitutes a stripping back
to powder and void
        Zeno, he cannot take my voice
and if I can never put these words on a page
I can at least speak from time to time and they will be heard
like when I tried to tell my students
about orality and song and aliterary subterfuge
and we awkwardly tenderly sang
Emily Dickinson poems
to the tune of well-known nursery rhymes
a trick I regret being told and which I regret relating now
but somehow, somehow it helps
Emily singing to herself –
the rhythm lulls the law away
the rhythm lulls the law
did I tell you I almost knew I had to leave
when I read that book by Lacan's daughter
not Sylvia Bataille's beautiful daughter but

the other one
the one who wrote and was ugly
whose muscles turned in on her
the one he would not acknowledge because she was ugly and she wrote
and her muscles turned in on her
to whom he gave the middle name 'Image'
after his theory of the mirror stage
we each have to shuck off *le nom du père*
all the moreso if you've never had one gaze back at you

    Dear Zeno
I've just got in
the other week Sophie came round
looked at my chart and said my 'wound' is in my eighth house
which is the house of sex and death
but ultimately and perhaps most pertinently
the house of 'trouble with other people's money'
perhaps my trouble is in identifying the line between my money
and other people's, in that mine so quickly becomes theirs
which is perhaps why it took me three years of therapy to be
    uncoerced
from supporting an abusive parent financially
I like to think this current paradox is the culmination of the wound
I have to pass through
rotating in coloured concentricities like representations of the inferno
in which case the paradox is a diagram is the cross-section of a wound
falsely squashed on a single plane
like microbes pressed between two slides
    Dear Zeno
as I said I don't have two disciplines to rub together
so how can I alchemically conjure interdisciplinarity?

I dread to think if I ever met Lord Kelvin or Adam Smith
would I pretend they were some kind of daddy?
daughterliness is a state I have aspired to and yet
it has usually wound up as some warped sexuality
or debt

    Dear Zeno, is a wound always pressed between two people like a
        page
or a banknote?

the willows on the common
are still on fire

the willows on the common are still on fire.
she lives in a combustible North.
memories, the engines
she doesn't want, keep firing blanks
at significance.
in the obsolete commons of crayons
and tarmac
children who resolve too soon to never
play with matches end
up setting themselves alight
with fervour or
goodwill. she keeps a sequin
in her palm; she knows
the sequin
is a girl seed,
a time capsule that must
be artificial, disc-like enough
to withstand its own heat

at weekends
she drives so far and long
to bring foil-wrapped cake to a mother
who will not eat
that her first big word
is 'outskirts'
as if the city
is a mesh of cheap tulle
and cigarette butts
that a mother can get
stitched into
and there never is an indication
of having reached the outskirts
but she is always looking for a sign

In our memoir on Spontaneous Generation

Everything combined to prevent the interference of air

On March 23rd we filled the shape represented

A most simple method of observing the deadly effect of air

To assure ourselves we filled two tubes

We cited a mineral medium

On April 9th we composed a liquid

This liquid had previously been left to herself

This liquid, the author says, had a feeble reaction

For the first few days she remained perfectly clear

Then began to grow turbid

On that same day we first observed a deposit

Between the mercury and the sides of the tube

Kept at summer heat, she speedily swarmed with organisms

By evening a tolerable activity had begun to manifest

On the fifth day a few bubbles betokened

On May 13th we refrained from impregnating

We examined a drop

She was less vigorous without having actually ceased

Under observation she seemed to languish

She showed every sign of intense unease and asphyxia

Although mobile at the articulations

After having lived without air

We concluded that she could not be suddenly exposed

We were forced to regard her as a distinct species

And have employed the vaguest nomenclature

Leaving her absolutely intact

> *She possesses unusual powers of resistance*

> *She may be brought to a state of dry dust, and be wafted about by winds*

NOTES

'Life without air' (*« la vie sans l'air »*) is how Louis Pasteur (1822–95) described the process of fermentation. Through a number of experiments – which included asphyxiating animals to death – he discovered that some organisms perish from a lack of oxygen, while others are able to thrive in states of airlessness (see 'The Physiological Theory of Fermentation: V. Another Example of Life Without Air', *Scientific Papers*, Harvard Classics, 1909–14). The coda is also based on these notes.

The epigraph is from Emily Dickinson's poem 'To fill a Gap' (546), *The Complete Poems of Emily Dickinson*, Thomas H. Johnson (ed.) (Faber and Faber, 1975).

'what Genie got' includes a line adapted from 1 Kings 17:6 (King James Version). Reproduced with permission of The Licensor through PLS-clear. The Licensor is Cambridge University Press.

understudies for air was published as a pamphlet of twenty-three poems by Sad Press in 2017. The poems proceed from the theory of Anaximenes (*c*. 586–526 BC) that air is the sole *arche*, the primary material from which all things are made.

'infrastructure air' proceeds from a line in Veronica Forrest-Thomson's poem 'In the Greenhouse' (*Collected Poems*, Shearsman Books, 2008).

The line 'she is vulnerable and subject to historical flux' is adapted from Barbara Newman's discussion of Ecclesia in *Sister of Wisdom: St. Hildegard's Theology of the Feminine* (University of California Press, 1987).

The first line of 'Life Without Air' borrows respectfully from Patrick Farmer. Empedocles (*c.* 494–434 BC) is said to have ended his life by throwing himself into Mount Etna.

Simone Weil's writing on parasites and divine love referred to in 'How to leave a marriage' can be found in her 'New York Notebook', collected in *First and Last Notebooks* (Oxford University Press, 1970).

The first line of 'ghosted' proceeds from a poem by CAConrad in *While Standing in Line for Death* (Wave Books, 2017).

'nothingness is the scene of wild activity' was written in response to *Nature's Optical Unconscious*, a lecture by Karen Barad in Edinburgh's Playfair Library in 2018.

'p value' was commissioned by Aniela Piasecka for her residency at Dance Base, Edinburgh, 2019.

'A Question for Zeno' is addressed to Zeno of Elea (*c.* 490–430 BC), most famous for his philosophical paradoxes. The book referred to in the poem is *A Father: Puzzle* by Sibylle Lacan (The MIT Press, 2019).

'the willows on the common are still on fire' was commissioned by Sean Edwards for the catalogue accompanying his exhibition *Undo Things Done* at the 2019 Venice Biennale.

ACKNOWLEDGEMENTS

This book is for my friends, who are my family. Thank you to Sophie, Dom, Aniela and Patrick: so much of this book wouldn't have come into existence without you.

I am grateful for the support of Rob, Alice and my Anglesey family – Philip, Hilly, Ben and Siân – whose care, kindness, rooms and homes enabled many of these poems to be written.

Thank you to the editors of *Poetry London*, *The White Review*, *Test Centre Magazine*, *Cumulus*, *Lighthouse*, *Poetry Review*, *The Weird Folds: Everyday Poems from the Anthropocene*, *Hotel*, *Mote* and *Tender*, where some of these poems first appeared.

Certain poems and texts were written as responses to artworks; my thanks to Sean Edwards and Aniela Piasecka for commissioning these pieces.

This book has benefitted from many people's time and care. I am grateful to my agent Karolina Sutton and to the team at Granta – most of all Rachael Allen, for her editorial vision and belief in this book from the outset. My unending thanks also to Patrick, Sophie, Rebecca, Geri and Catriona, for insightful readings and careful feedback on the manuscript.